Putting Jesus First

Jesus Calling® Bible Study Series

Volume 1: Experiencing God's Presence

Volume 2: Trusting in Christ

Volume 3: Receiving Christ's Hope

Volume 4: Living a Life of Worship

Volume 5: Giving Thanks to God

Volume 6: Living with God's Courage

Volume 7: Dwelling in God's Peace

Volume 8: Putting Jesus First

Jesus Calling® Bible Study Series

Putting Jesus First

Eight Sessions

Sarah Young

with Karen Lee-Thorp

Thomas Nelson
Since 1798

Published in Nashville, Tennessee, by Thomas Nelson. Thomas Nelson is a registered trademark of HarperCollins Christian Publishing, Inc.

ISBN 978-0-310-08370-2

First Printing July 2017 / Printed in the United States of America

CONTENTS

INTRODUCTION

Sometimes our busy and difficult lives give us the impression that God is silent. We cry out to Him, but our feelings tell us that He isn't answering our prayers. In this, our feelings are incorrect. God hears the prayers of His children and speaks right into the situations in which we find ourselves. The trouble is that our lives are often too hectic, our minds too distracted, for us to take in what He offers.

This *Jesus Calling* Bible study is designed to help individuals and groups meditate on the words of Scripture and hear them not just as words said to people long ago but as words said to us today in the here and now. The goal is to help the heart open up and respond to what the mind reads—to encounter the living God as He speaks through the Scriptures. The writer to the Hebrews tells us:

> In the past God spoke to our ancestors through the prophets at many times and in various ways, but in these last days he has spoken to us by his Son, whom he appointed heir of all things, and through whom also he made the universe. The Son is the radiance of God's glory and the exact representation of his being, sustaining all things by his powerful word.
>
> —HEBREWS 1:1–3

God has spoken to us through His Son, Jesus Christ. The New Testament gives us the chance to walk with Jesus, see what He does, and hear Him speak into the sometimes confusing situations in which we find ourselves. The Old Testament tells us the story of how God prepared a people to be the family of Jesus, and in the experiences of those men and women we find our own lives mirrored.

THE GOAL OF THIS SERIES

The *Jesus Calling Bible Study Series* offers you a chance to lay down your cares, enter God's Presence, and hear Him speak through His Word. You will get to spend some time silently studying a passage of Scripture, and then, if you're meeting with a group, openly sharing your insights and hearing what others discovered. You'll also get to discuss excerpts from the *Jesus Calling* devotional that relate to the themes of the Bible passages. In this way, you will learn how to better make space in your life for the Spirit of God to speak to you through the Word of God and the people of God.

THE FLOW OF EACH SESSION

Each session of this study guide contains the following elements:

- CONSIDER IT. The two questions in this opening section serve as an icebreaker to help you start thinking about the theme of the session, connecting it to your own past or present experience and allowing you to get to know the others in your group more deeply. If you've had a busy day and your mind is full of distractions, these questions can help you better focus.

- EXPERIENCE IT. Here you will find two readings from *Jesus Calling* along with some questions for reflection. This is your chance to talk with others about the biblical principles found within the *Jesus Calling* devotions. Can you relate to what each reading describes? What insights from God's Word does it illuminate? What does it motivate you to do? This section will assist you in applying these biblical principles to your everyday habits.

- STUDY IT. Next you'll explore a Scripture passage connected to the session topic and the readings from *Jesus Calling*. You will not only analyze these Bible passages but also pray through them in ways designed to engage your heart and your head. You'll first talk with your group about what the verse or verses mean and then spend several minutes in silence, letting God speak into your life through His Word.

- LIVE IT. Finally, you will find five days' worth of suggested Scripture passages that you can pray through on your own during the week. Suggested questions for additional study and reflection are provided.

FOR LEADERS

If you are leading a group through this study guide, please see the Leader's Notes at the end of the guide. You'll find background on the design of the study as well as suggested answers for some of the study questions.

SESSION 1

Putting Jesus First in Times of Busyness

Consider It

Back in the 1930s, economist John Maynard Keynes predicted that future generations would work only about fifteen hours each week. Keynes had witnessed technological advances shrink the workday in his time, and he had every reason to believe this trend would continue. Keynes was partly right—leisure time for people in developed countries has, on average, steadily increased over the years. But today, people *feel* busier than ever.

What's the reason for this? Part of the problem seems to stem from the fact that our society evaluates us based on how much we are able to produce in a given day. We feel pressured to make every moment count—and fill every moment with a task to complete. As a result, most of us are crazy busy trying to satisfy all the demands.

What we desperately need is to ground ourselves in Jesus' standard for evaluating our lives. He's not all about how much we produce but about how much we love Him and other people. Putting Jesus first means putting Him first in the way we use our time. But how is that possible, given the way people around us (and a voice inside us) press us to accomplish a superhuman amount of things each day? This is what we will explore during this first session.

1. *What does a typical day look like for you?*

2. *Why do you suppose we tend to value busyness in our society?*

Experience It

"Approach this day with awareness of who is Boss. As you make plans for the day, remember that it is I who orchestrate the events of your life. On days when things go smoothly, according to your plans, you may be unaware of My sovereign Presence. On days when your plans are thwarted, be on the lookout for Me! I may be doing something important in your life, something quite different from what you expected. It is essential at such times to stay in communication with Me, accepting My way as better than yours. Don't try to figure out what is happening. Simply trust Me and thank Me in advance for the good that will come out of it all. *I know the plans I have for you, and they are good.*"

—From *Jesus Calling*, January 20

3. ***What are some possible implications of recognizing Jesus as your boss? How could this perspective change your outlook on the tasks you strive to do each day?***

4. ***What is the value of being on the lookout for Christ when your plans are thwarted?***

"Be still in My Presence, even though countless tasks clamor for your attention. Nothing is as important as spending time with Me. While you wait in My Presence, I do My best work within you: *transforming you by the renewing of your mind*. If you skimp on this time with Me, you may plunge headlong into the wrong activities, missing the richness of what I have planned for you.

"Do not seek Me primarily for what I can give you. Remember that I, the Giver, am infinitely greater than any gift I might impart to you. Though I delight in blessing My children, I am deeply grieved when My blessings become idols in their hearts. Anything can be an idol if it distracts you from Me as your *First Love*. When I am the ultimate Desire of your heart, you are safe from the danger of idolatry. As you wait in My Presence, enjoy the greatest gift of all: *Christ in you, the hope of Glory*!"

—From *Jesus Calling*, March 27

5. ***Is it difficult for you to make space in your life to be still in Jesus' presence? Why would this be important? What would help you create this space in the midst of a hectic day?***

6. ***What's the difference between seeking Jesus for what He can give you and seeking Him for Himself? How can you know if you are seeking Him just for His gifts?***

Study It

Read aloud the following passage from Luke 10:38–42. As you read, note that hospitality was considered a sacred responsibility in the culture of the time, and women in particular were expected to provide it. Furthermore, it was unheard of for a woman to sit at a rabbi's feet as a disciple to learn from him. Jesus was radical in allowing a woman to do what Mary did—and even more radical for *encouraging* her to do it.

> [38] As Jesus and his disciples were on their way, he came to a village where a woman named Martha opened her home to him. [39] She had a sister called Mary, who sat at the Lord's feet listening to what he said. [40] But Martha was distracted by all the preparations that had to be made. She came to him and asked, "Lord, don't you care that my sister has left me to do the work by myself? Tell her to help me!"
>
> [41] "Martha, Martha," the Lord answered, "you are worried and upset about many things, [42] but few things are needed—or indeed only one. Mary has chosen what is better, and it will not be taken away from her."

7. ***What did Martha think it meant to put Jesus first? What do you think of her view?***

8. ***What did Mary think it meant to put Jesus first? What do you think of her view?***

9. *How would you evaluate your own priorities in light of this account? What does it say to those of us with busy and hectic lives?*

10. *How, in practice, do you carve out time for Jesus in your hectic life? Is it possible for you to listen less to the voices that demand productivity and more to Jesus' voice?*

11. *Take two minutes of silence to reread the passage, looking for a sentence, phrase, or even one word that stands out as something Jesus may want you to focus on in your life. If you're meeting with a group, the leader will keep track of time. At the end of two minutes, you may share with the group the word or phrase that came to you in the silence.*

12. *Read the passage aloud again. Take another two minutes of silence, prayerfully considering what response God might want you to make to what you have read in His Word. If you're meeting with a group, the leader will again keep track of time. At the end of two minutes, you may share with the group what came to you in the silence if you wish.*

13. *If you're meeting with a group, how can the members pray for you? If you're using this study on your own, what would you like to say to God right now?*

LIVE IT

At the end of each session you'll find suggested Scripture readings for spending time alone with God during five days of the coming week. This week, the theme of each reading will focus on putting Jesus first in the midst of your busy life. Read each passage slowly, pausing to think about what is being said. Rather than approaching this as an assignment to complete, think of it as an opportunity to meet with the One who loves you most. Use any of the questions that are helpful.

Day 1

Read Revelation 2:1–5. For what good things does Jesus praise the church in Ephesus?

Look closely at verse 4. As a Christian, how would you know if you had lost your "first love"—the love you had for Jesus back in your early days of knowing Him? What would be the telltale signs?

What steps would you need to take to restore that first-love relationship with Jesus?

Tell Jesus today that you want to love Him with a love that never fades over time. Ask Him to show you ways for fostering that deep kind of love for Him.

Day 2

Read Isaiah 30:15–18. Why are repentance and rest so important?

What would quietness and trust look like in your life today?

It's easy to get caught up in a whirlwind of activity, whether it's fleeing from enemies, as in this passage, or trying to get a million things done. What is the net result of trying to do everything in your own strength? What does God long to do for those who love Him?

Consider what it would look like if you made resting in God and relying on His strength a continual pattern for your life. Take a few minutes today to step away from your schedule, put Him first, and just spend time resting in His presence.

Day 3

Read Exodus 33:12–14. What promise did God give when Moses expressed that he was overwhelmed with the task before him? How would this promise make a difference in your life as a follower of Christ?

What gets in the way of rest for you? How can God's presence help with those obstacles?

Why is it essential to put Jesus first in order to experience His rest?

Ask Jesus to make you more aware of His presence as you go through your day—and to put Him first in your choices.

Day 4

Read Psalm 40:16–17. Why does it make sense that those who truly seek Jesus will rejoice and be glad in Him? How does putting Him first lead to joy?

What is the value of seeing yourself as poor and needy when you go to God? Why is that better than going to Him with the attitude that you are strong and capable of achieving whatever you set your mind to do?

What is the primary challenge you face in seeking to put Jesus first today? How can Jesus help you with that challenge?

Make a renewed decision to seek Jesus throughout your day. Ask Him to show you what that will involve and what priorities you need to shift in your schedule.

Day 5

Read Psalm 119:10–11. What will it look like for you to seek Jesus with all your heart in this day?

What is the connection between Jesus' commands to love God and others and putting Him first during a full day?

Why is it so important to hide God's Word in your heart before you venture out into a busy day?

Take a few minutes to hide verse 10 in your heart, and repeat it to yourself throughout the day. Look for ways to apply it as you do tasks.

SESSION 2

Putting Jesus First in Times of Anxiety

Consider It

Tune in to any newscast and it won't take long to realize the world is a scary, uncertain place. Whether it's hurricanes ravaging the coastline, outbreaks of disease in populated areas, or new threats of conflict across the world, the news stories that can produce panic within us just seem to keep on coming. We are more connected to events in our world today than ever before—and more nervous and on edge as a result.

Anxiety plagues so many of us today that it's almost become a way of life. We worry about our finances, our security, our health—and about the security, health, and welfare of our loved ones. We worry about losing the things we love. We worry about stepping into a new situation. We worry about what the future has in store for us. And as soon as we get past one anxiety-producing moment, the next one appears on the horizon.

How do we overcome this temptation to worry? By consciously putting Jesus first in our thoughts and actions and trusting that He is in control of the world. Jesus wants to give us a new perspective that will melt our anxieties away. In this session, we will listen to His voice and explore what He has to say about letting go of our worries.

1. *Do you tend to worry about things? If so, what are some recent things you've been worried about? If not, how do you choose to deal with challenges or unknown situations?*

2. *Why do you think the tendency to worry is so strong in people?*

EXPERIENCE IT

"Seek My Face, and you will find more than you ever dreamed possible. *Let Me displace worry at the center of your being.* I am like a supersaturated cloud, showering Peace into the pool of your mind. My Nature is to bless. Your nature is to receive with thanksgiving. This is a true fit, designed before the foundation of the world. Glorify Me by receiving My blessings gratefully.

"I am the goal of all your searching. *When you seek Me, you find Me* and are satisfied. When lesser goals capture your attention, I fade into the background of your life. I am still there, watching and waiting, but you function as if you were alone. Actually, My Light shines on every situation you will ever face. Live radiantly by expanding your focus to include Me in all your moments. Let nothing dampen your search for Me."

—FROM *JESUS CALLING*, JANUARY 19

3. ***How do you go about letting Jesus displace your worries?***

4. ***What do you think are some of the benefits of seeking Jesus? If you are a believer, how have you experienced these benefits?***

"You are on the path of My choosing. There is no randomness about your life. Here and Now comprise the coordinates of your daily life. Most people let their moments slip through their fingers, half-lived. They avoid the present by worrying about the future or longing for a better time and place. They forget that they are creatures who are subject to the limitations of time and space. They forget their Creator, who walks with them only in the present.

"Every moment is alive with My glorious Presence, to those whose hearts are intimately connected with Mine. As you give yourself more and more to a life of constant communion with Me, you will find that you simply have no time for worry. Thus, you are freed to let My Spirit direct your steps, enabling you to walk along *the path of Peace*."

—From *Jesus Calling*, May 1

5. ***What are some good reasons for shedding your worry?***

6. ***Are you more likely to dwell on the past, worry about the future, or focus on the present? Explain.***

Study It

Read aloud the following passage from Matthew 6:25–34. These verses comprise part of what is known as the Sermon on the Mount, which is a group of teachings that Jesus delivered to the crowds who came to hear Him early in His ministry. As you read, focus on what Jesus says about the futility of worry and why we, as God's children, can trust that He will always care for us.

> [25] "Therefore I tell you, do not worry about your life, what you will eat or drink; or about your body, what you will wear. Is not life more than food, and the body more than clothes? [26] Look at the birds of the air; they do not sow or reap or store away in barns, and yet your heavenly Father feeds them. Are you not much more valuable than they? [27] Can any one of you by worrying add a single hour to your life?
>
> [28] "And why do you worry about clothes? See how the flowers of the field grow. They do not labor or spin. [29] Yet I tell you that not even Solomon in all his splendor was dressed like one of these. [30] If that is how God clothes the grass of the field, which is here today and tomorrow is thrown into the fire, will he not much more clothe you—you of little faith? [31] So do not worry, saying, 'What shall we eat?' or 'What shall we drink?' or 'What shall we wear?' [32] For the pagans run after all these things, and your heavenly Father knows that you need them. [33] But seek first his kingdom and his righteousness, and all these things will be given to you as well. [34] Therefore do not worry about tomorrow, for tomorrow will worry about itself. Each day has enough trouble of its own."

7. ***What reasons does Jesus offer for why those who belong to God's family don't need to worry?***

8. ***What does it mean to "seek first" God's kingdom and His righteousness? How can you put that into practice in your life?***

9. ***What are some kingdom activities that demonstrate putting Jesus first, ahead of your worries about your own needs? (See, for example, Matthew 5:43–48 and 25:34–40.)***

10. ***What would putting Jesus first, ahead of your worries, look like for you this week?***

11. *Take two minutes of silence to reread the passage, looking for a sentence, phrase, or even one word that stands out as something Jesus may want you to focus on in your life. If you're meeting with a group, the leader will keep track of time. At the end of two minutes, you may share with the group the word or phrase that came to you in the silence.*

12. *Read the passage aloud again. Take another two minutes of silence, prayerfully considering what response God might want you to make to what you have read in His Word. If you're meeting with a group, the leader will again keep track of time. At the end of two minutes, you may share with the group what came to you in the silence if you wish.*

13. *If you're meeting with a group, how can the members pray for you? If you're using this study on your own, what would you like to say to God right now?*

Live It

The theme of this week's daily Scripture readings is on putting Jesus first in your anxious times and letting go of worry. Read each passage slowly, pausing to think about what is being said. Rather than approaching this as an assignment to complete, think of it as an opportunity to meet with the One who loves you most. Use any of the questions that are helpful.

Day 1

Read Philippians 4:6–7. What does this passage state about putting Jesus first? How is that an alternative to anxiety?

Why do you think this is a good antidote to worry?

How can you put the teachings of this passage into practice today?

Present your requests to God today with thanksgiving. As His son or daughter, choose to trust Him to take care of your needs, and don't anxiously rehearse the things you've prayed for. Really leave them in His hands.

Day 2

Read Psalm 63:1. How do you go about earnestly seeking Jesus?

In what sense do you live in a "dry and parched land where there is no water"?

Do you thirst for Jesus? Or are you more aware of thirsting for other things? Explain.

Earnestly seek Jesus today. Consider committing Psalm 63:1 to memory so you can pray it throughout the day.

Day 3

Read Psalm 63:2–5. As a follower of Christ, in what ways have you beheld God's power and glory in your life?

Do you believe that Jesus' love is better than life? What are the signs of that in the way you live?

In what ways is Jesus more satisfying than "the richest of foods"?

Look for the ways that God is revealing His power and glory to you as you go about your day.

Day 4

Read Psalm 63:6–8. What does it mean to keep God foremost in your thoughts "through the watches of the night"? Do you think this is meant to be taken literally? Why or why not? What would it take for you to make God that much of a priority?

What is the psalmist trying to convey when he says, "I sing in the shadow of your wings" (verse 7)?

What is the psalmist trying to convey when he says "your right hand upholds me" (verse 8)?

If you have trouble sleeping because of worry, in spite of being a child of God, try praising and praying to Jesus in the evening before you go to bed. And if you find yourself awake at night, take that opportunity to express grateful prayers to God.

Day 5

Read Psalm 63:9–11. Hopefully you don't have human enemies who are seeking to kill you, but who are the Christian's spiritual enemies? What do these verses say about them?

How easy is it to have confidence as a believer that this is what will happen to your enemies? Why?

What reasons for putting Jesus first do these verses offer?

Rejoice in Jesus today, and whenever you are tempted to worry about your circumstances, remind yourself that, because you have trusted in Him, He is triumphing over your enemies.

SESSION 3

Putting Jesus First in Times of Fear

Consider It

King David lived in fearful times. He had many enemies that were after him throughout his life, and his psalms are filled with prayers to God for protection. Again and again we find David uttering cries such as, "Save me, O God, by your name. . . . Arrogant foes are attacking me" (Psalm 54:1, 3), and "Rescue me, Lord, from evildoers" (Psalm 140:1).

Today our human enemies may be harder to spot. There are terrorists who wish us ill, or we may have someone in our lives—a coworker perhaps—who wants to bring us down. Even if we don't have *human* enemies, we know that Satan and his minions want to drive a wedge between us and God and drag us into sin.

When we're aware of a threat, it's easy to let it fill our vision and blot out everything else. But David and the other psalmists continually point us back to the Lord, urging us to put Him first even when we face real malice. In this session, we'll try to adopt a psalmist's mindset.

1. *What are some "threats" in the world today? How do those threats impact your life?*

2. *What do you do when you encounter a situation that causes you fear? How do you tend to handle the stress you feel?*

EXPERIENCE IT

"Make Me your focal point as you move through this day. Just as a spinning ballerina must keep returning her eyes to a given point to maintain her balance, so you must keep returning your focus to Me. Circumstances are in flux, and the world seems to be whirling around you. The only way to keep your balance is to *fix your eyes on Me*, the One who never changes. If you gaze too long at your circumstances, you will become dizzy and confused. Look to Me, refreshing yourself in My Presence, and your steps will be steady and sure."

—FROM *JESUS CALLING*, APRIL 25

3. ***Why does gazing too long at your circumstances tend to have a dizzying or confusing effect? Have you ever experienced this? If so, describe your experience.***

4. ***How would you go about making Jesus the focal point of your day?***

"I want to be Central in your entire being. When your focus is firmly on Me, My Peace displaces fears and worries. They will encircle you, seeking entrance, so you must stay alert. Let trust and thankfulness stand

> guard, turning back fear before it can gain a foothold. *There is no fear in My Love*, which shines on you continually. Sit quietly in My Love-Light while I bless you with radiant Peace. Turn your whole being to trusting and loving Me."
>
> —From *Jesus Calling*, June 3

5. ***When have your fears surrounded you and tried to intrude on the peace Jesus has given you as one of His own?***

6. ***How do trust and thankfulness help you put Jesus first?***

Study It

Read aloud the following passage from Psalm 71:1–24. While the author of this psalm is unknown, many believe it was either written by the prophet Jeremiah or by King David, when he fled Jerusalem during the time of Absalom's rebellion (see 2 Samuel 15). What is clear is that the author is an older individual who has gone through many fearful times in his life—but is still able to fully put his trust in the Lord in spite of these trials.

[1] In you, LORD, I have taken refuge;
let me never be put to shame.
[2] In your righteousness, rescue me and deliver me;
turn your ear to me and save me.
[3] Be my rock of refuge,
to which I can always go;
give the command to save me,
for you are my rock and my fortress.
[4] Deliver me, my God, from the hand of the wicked,
from the grasp of those who are evil and cruel.
[5] For you have been my hope, Sovereign LORD,
my confidence since my youth.
[6] From birth I have relied on you;
you brought me forth from my mother's womb.
I will ever praise you.
[7] I have become a sign to many;
you are my strong refuge.
[8] My mouth is filled with your praise,
declaring your splendor all day long.
[9] Do not cast me away when I am old;
do not forsake me when my strength is gone.
[10] For my enemies speak against me;
those who wait to kill me conspire together.
[11] They say, "God has forsaken him;
pursue him and seize him,
for no one will rescue him."
[12] Do not be far from me, my God;
come quickly, God, to help me.
[13] May my accusers perish in shame;
may those who want to harm me
be covered with scorn and disgrace.
[14] As for me, I will always have hope;
I will praise you more and more.

[15] My mouth will tell of your righteous deeds,
of your saving acts all day long—
though I know not how to relate them all.
[16] I will come and proclaim your mighty acts, Sovereign Lord;
I will proclaim your righteous deeds, yours alone.
[17] Since my youth, God, you have taught me,
and to this day I declare your marvelous deeds.
[18] Even when I am old and gray,
do not forsake me, my God,
till I declare your power to the next generation,
your mighty acts to all who are to come.
[19] Your righteousness, God, reaches to the heavens,
you who have done great things.
Who is like you, God?
[20] Though you have made me see troubles,
many and bitter,
you will restore my life again;
from the depths of the earth
you will again bring me up.
[21] You will increase my honor
and comfort me once more.
[22] I will praise you with the harp
for your faithfulness, my God;
I will sing praise to you with the lyre,
Holy One of Israel.
[23] My lips will shout for joy
when I sing praise to you—
I whom you have delivered.
[24] My tongue will tell of your righteous acts
all day long,
for those who wanted to harm me
have been put to shame and confusion.

7. *What does the psalmist ask God to do in verses 1–4 and verse 9?*

8. *Why is the psalmist confident that God will come through for him (see verses 5–6)? Can you say the same in your times of fear? Explain.*

9. *The psalmist speaks of hope in verses 5 and 14. Biblical hope is not just "wishful thinking" but a confident expectation that what God promised will come to pass. What do you hope for? Why is it important to have Jesus as the focus of your hope during fearful times?*

10. *The psalmist says several times that he will proclaim God's mighty deeds (see verses 15–18). What was he referring to here? Why is it important to remember God's mighty acts in the past when you are facing times of fear?*

11. *Take two minutes of silence to reread the passage, looking for a sentence, phrase, or even one word that stands out as something Jesus may want you to focus on in your life. If you're meeting with a group, the leader will keep track of time. At the end of two minutes, you may share with the group the word or phrase that came to you in the silence.*

12. *Read the passage aloud again. Take another two minutes of silence, prayerfully considering what response God might want you to make to what you have read in His Word. If you're meeting with a group, the leader will again keep track of time. At the end of two minutes, you may share with the group what came to you in the silence if you wish.*

13. ***If you're meeting with a group, how can the members pray for you? If you're using this study on your own, what would you like to say to God right now?***

LIVE IT

This week's daily Scripture readings focus on putting Jesus first during those fearful times when you feel under threat. Read each passage slowly, pausing to think about what is being said. Rather than approaching this as an assignment to complete, think of it as an opportunity to meet with the One who loves you most. Use any of the questions that are helpful.

Day 1

Read Psalm 27:1–3. For a Christian, what does it mean to say that the Lord is your light?

What other reasons for not being afraid do these verses offer to believers in Christ?

How are these verses a motivation to put Jesus first in all that you do?

Choose a line from these verses to reflect on throughout your day. Remember that because Jesus is every believer's light and salvation, you have nothing to fear in this world if you have given your life over to Him.

Day 2

Read Psalm 27:4–6. In these verses, David prays for nothing more than to dwell in the Lord's house. How can you dwell in the Lord's house today?

How does dwelling in the Lord's house keep the people of God safe in "the day of trouble"?

What confidence does David express in God's deliverance from his trials?

Choose to dwell with Jesus today. Ask Him to help you do this and to keep you safe there.

Day 3

Read Psalm 27:7–9. As a Christian, do you believe Jesus hears your voice when you call? What helps you to believe this? What gets in the way?

How can you "seek his face" (verse 8) today? What does this look like in your life?

How is putting Jesus first related to the confidence that He will never hide His face from those who put their trust in Him?

Seek Jesus' face today. Look for an opportunity to put Him first, ahead of other agendas.

Day 4

Read Psalm 27:10–12. Have your father or mother let you down? How have you seen the Lord through the filter of your parents? How is He a better parent?

How does Jesus teach you His way?

Who are the "false witnesses" that rise up against you as a follower of Christ? Of what can you be confident regarding them, if Jesus is number one in your life?

Rehearse to yourself the ways in which the Lord is a better parent than any earthly parent. Let yourself sink into that confidence as a child of God when you're tempted to be afraid today.

Day 5

Read Psalm 27:13–14. What does it mean to wait for the Lord?

Why does it take courage to wait for Him?

How confident are you that you will see the goodness of the Lord in the land of the living? Why? Why should you have that confidence if you're a believer in Christ?

Make the phrase "wait for the Lord" the one that rules your day today. Bring it to mind whenever you have to choose between putting Jesus first or putting something (or someone) else first. Especially bring it to mind when you're tempted to be afraid rather than trusting Him.

SESSION 4

Putting Jesus First in Times of Uncertainty

CONSIDER IT

As believers in Christ, we all want to know God's will for our lives—especially when we are going through times of uncertainty and have to make important decisions that will affect our future. During such moments, we often think of pursuing God's will in terms of the "big picture." We ask ourselves questions such as, *What career path should I follow? What church should I attend? Who should I marry? Does God want me to be a stay-at-home mother? How many children should I have? Should I homeschool them?*

While it is important to seek God's answers to these big-picture questions, we have to remember that His Word tells us to "look to the LORD and his strength; seek his face always" (1 Chronicles 16:11) and "be joyful in hope, patient in affliction, faithful in prayer" (Romans 12:12). The key to knowing God's will during uncertain times when big decisions need to be made comes from patiently and persistently seeking His will in the smaller areas of life—day by day and hour by hour. In this session, we'll look at what the Bible says about seeking God's wisdom each day and how putting Him first will lead us through uncertain times.

1. ***What is an area in which you are seeking to discern Jesus' will for your life? Or what is a matter about which you need wisdom?***

2. ***What are some uncertainties that you are facing in your future? What habits are you developing now to help you know God's direction?***

Experience It

"I am your Lord! Seek Me as Friend and Lover of your soul, but remember that I am also King of kings—sovereign over all. You can make some plans as you gaze into the day that stretches out before you. But you need to hold those plans tentatively, anticipating that I may have other ideas. The most important thing to determine is what to do right now. Instead of scanning the horizon of your life, looking for things that need to be done, concentrate on the task before you and the One who never leaves your side. Let everything else fade into the background. This will unclutter your mind, allowing Me to occupy more and more of your consciousness.

"Trust Me to show you what to do when you have finished what you are doing now. I will guide you step by step as you bend your will to Mine. Thus you stay close to Me on the *path of Peace*."

—From *Jesus Calling*, May 16

3. ***Do you tend to scan the horizon of your life and look for things you can do to get to where you think you need to be? What are some problems with this approach?***

4. ***How easy or difficult is it for you to trust Jesus with the next step instead of planning everything out in detail? Why do you think God often reveals His plan one step at a time?***

"Seek to please Me above all else. Let that goal be your focal point as you go through this day. Such a mind-set will protect you from scattering your energy to the winds. The free will I bestowed on you comes with awesome responsibility. Each day presents you with choice after choice. Many of these decisions you ignore and thus make by default. Without a focal point to guide you, you can easily lose your way. That's why it is so important to stay in communication with Me, living in thankful awareness of My Presence.

"You inhabit a fallen, disjointed world, where things are constantly unraveling around the edges. Only a vibrant relationship with Me can keep you from coming unraveled too."

—From *Jesus Calling*, September 18

5. ***What opportunities have you had this week to please Jesus above all else? How does thinking about your life in terms of pleasing God first help you to discern His will as you make choices?***

6. ***What are some things that get in the way of paying attention to Jesus' guidance in the small things? How can you overcome these obstacles?***

Study It

Read aloud the following passage from Job 28:1–28. Job was a man who had lost all his children, his wealth, and his health. Some of his friends had said that God must be punishing him for sins he committed, but Job had been steadfast in defending his integrity. In this chapter, Job speaks of wisdom, which in biblical terms is the God-given ability to think and do rightly in the practical areas of life. Notice how the poem piles up images to make its point so that the last verse really stands out.

[1] There is a mine for silver
and a place where gold is refined.
[2] Iron is taken from the earth,
and copper is smelted from ore.
[3] Mortals put an end to the darkness;
they search out the farthest recesses
for ore in the blackest darkness.
[4] Far from human dwellings they cut a shaft,
in places untouched by human feet;
far from other people they dangle and sway.
[5] The earth, from which food comes,
is transformed below as by fire;
[6] lapis lazuli comes from its rocks,
and its dust contains nuggets of gold.
[7] No bird of prey knows that hidden path,
no falcon's eye has seen it.
[8] Proud beasts do not set foot on it,
and no lion prowls there.
[9] People assault the flinty rock with their hands
and lay bare the roots of the mountains.
[10] They tunnel through the rock;
their eyes see all its treasures.
[11] They search the sources of the rivers

and bring hidden things to light.
[12] But where can wisdom be found?
Where does understanding dwell?
[13] No mortal comprehends its worth;
it cannot be found in the land of the living.
[14] The deep says, "It is not in me";
the sea says, "It is not with me."
[15] It cannot be bought with the finest gold,
nor can its price be weighed out in silver.
[16] It cannot be bought with the gold of Ophir,
with precious onyx or lapis lazuli.
[17] Neither gold nor crystal can compare with it,
nor can it be had for jewels of gold.
[18] Coral and jasper are not worthy of mention;
the price of wisdom is beyond rubies.
[19] The topaz of Cush cannot compare with it;
it cannot be bought with pure gold.
[20] Where then does wisdom come from?
Where does understanding dwell?
[21] It is hidden from the eyes of every living thing,
concealed even from the birds in the sky.
[22] Destruction and Death say,
"Only a rumor of it has reached our ears."
[23] God understands the way to it
and he alone knows where it dwells,
[24] for he views the ends of the earth
and sees everything under the heavens.
[25] When he established the force of the wind
and measured out the waters,
[26] when he made a decree for the rain
and a path for the thunderstorm,
[27] then he looked at wisdom and appraised it;
he confirmed it and tested it.

[28] And he said to the human race,
"The fear of the Lord—that is wisdom,
and to shun evil is understanding."

7. ***What point is Job making about wisdom in verses 1–13? Why do you think he uses so many verses to convey this insight?***

8. ***What does Job say about the value of wisdom in verses 13–19? Why do you think he uses so many verses to make this point?***

9. ***In verse 28, Job tells us that the "fear of the Lord" leads to wisdom. What does it mean to fear the Lord? How does fearing the Lord lead His people to wisdom in times of uncertainty?***

10. *How should the fear of the Lord affect the way you think about acquiring wisdom and discerning Jesus' will in the midst of life's uncertainties?*

11. *Take two minutes of silence to reread the passage, looking for a sentence, phrase, or even one word that stands out as something Jesus may want you to focus on in your life. If you're meeting with a group, the leader will keep track of time. At the end of two minutes, you may share with the group the word or phrase that came to you in the silence.*

12. *Read the passage aloud again. Take another two minutes of silence, prayerfully considering what response God might want you to make to what you have read in His Word. If you're meeting with a group, the leader will again keep track of time. At the end of two minutes, you may share with the group what came to you in the silence if you wish.*

13. ***If you're meeting with a group, how can the members pray for you? If you're using this study on your own, what would you like to say to God right now?***

LIVE IT

The theme of this week's daily Scripture readings is putting Jesus first by seeking His wisdom in times of uncertainty. Read each passage slowly, pausing to think about what is being said. Rather than approaching this as an assignment to complete, think of it as an opportunity to meet with the One who loves you most. Use any of the questions that are helpful.

Day 1

Read James 1:5–6. According to this passage, how does a person acquire wisdom?

Why is it significant that God generously supplies His people with wisdom without condemning them for their need of it?

How does James say believers in Christ should ask for God's wisdom? Why is this important?

If you are facing times of uncertainty today, admit to Jesus those areas where you need wisdom. Also, ask Him to give you wisdom even in the areas where you don't know you need it!

Day 2

Read Proverbs 19:21. What does this proverb say about putting Jesus first?

What plans do you need to submit to the Lord to receive His verdict on them?

When have you seen the truth of this proverb played out in your life as a believer in Christ? How did that experience affect your intimacy with Jesus during your uncertain times?

Submit your plans for today to Jesus, and ask Him to guide you in His purposes.

Day 3

Read Psalm 34:8–14. What wise counsel does this passage offer for facing those times in life that are filled with dangers and uncertainties?

The psalmist speaks of fearing the Lord and seeking the Lord (see verses 10–11). Is it surprising to you that these two things go together? Why or why not? How could fearing the Lord motivate you to seek the Lord?

How are the instructions in verses 13–14 relevant to putting Jesus first in your daily life?

Look for a way to pursue doing good today out of a desire to be close to Jesus.

Day 4

Read Proverbs 2:1–5. How does the speaker urge his son to treat the pursuit of wisdom? Can it be done halfheartedly? Why or why not?

How do you go about searching for wisdom as hidden treasure? What sources would you draw on, and how would you handle them?

Why is wisdom so valuable? Do you treat it as valuable? If so, how?

Ask Jesus to open your eyes to His wisdom in the Scriptures and in your daily life.

Day 5

Read Proverbs 2:6–8. When the writer says the Lord "holds success in store for the upright" (verse 7), he doesn't mean that those who lead godly lives will be successful in everything they attempt. Rather, he means that, as a general rule, the upright are more likely to succeed in life. Does that motivate you to lead a godly life? Or do you expect a more ironclad guarantee? Why?

The Lord "protects the way of his faithful ones" (verse 8) during times of uncertainty. What opportunities have you had recently to be faithful to Him as His child?

What practical takeaways have you learned this week about seeking the Lord's wisdom when you're facing uncertainties?

Take one step today toward pursuing wisdom by consulting Jesus in all you do, *before* you act.

SESSION 5

Putting Jesus First in Times of Longing

Consider It

As we discussed in a prior session, King David was a man who had many enemies and was often on the run for his life. At one point, he was forced to flee because his own son was after his throne. Yet even in these dire circumstances, David wrote psalms about his longing to be with the Lord: "You, God, are my God . . . I thirst for you, my whole being longs for you, in a dry and parched land where there is no water" (Psalm 63:1).

Later, during the Sermon on the Mount, Jesus would announce, "Blessed are those who hunger and thirst for righteousness, for they will be filled" (Matthew 5:6). And He would say to a Samaritan woman He met at a well, "Everyone who drinks this water will be thirsty again, but whoever drinks the water I give them will never thirst. Indeed, the water I give them will become in them a spring of water welling up to eternal life" (John 4:13–14).

We are a thirsty people . . . a people with a deep longing in our hearts. We can seek to fulfill those longings with the "water" of this world—possessions, money, relationships—but those things will never ultimately satisfy us. It is only when we fill our longings with the "living water" of Christ that we will attain the fulfillment we seek. So, while we don't need to become people without desires, we do need to be people who know that our deepest desire is for Jesus Himself. In this session, we'll lean into our longing to see just that.

1. ***What are some longings people typically have? What do people tend to thirst for in life?***

2. ***What are some ways people try to fulfill these needs outside of God?***

EXPERIENCE IT

"Worship Me only. I am *King of kings and Lord of lords, dwelling in unapproachable Light*. I am taking care of you! I am not only committed to caring for you, but I am also absolutely capable of doing so. Rest in Me, My weary one, for this is a form of worship.

"Though self-flagellation has gone out of style, many of My children drive themselves like racehorses. They whip themselves into action, ignoring how exhausted they are. They forget that I am sovereign and that *My ways are higher* than theirs. Underneath their driven service, they may secretly resent Me as a harsh taskmaster. Their worship of Me is lukewarm because I am no longer their *First Love*.

"My invitation never changes: *Come to Me, all you who are weary, and I will give you rest*. Worship Me by resting peacefully in My Presence."

—FROM *JESUS CALLING*, OCTOBER 1

3. ***How could resting in Jesus be a form of worship? How can this fill your longings?***

4. ***Do you drive yourself like a racehorse? How much of your downtime is devoted to resting in Jesus, and how much is devoted to pursuing other things?***

"Come to Me when you are hurting, and I will soothe your pain. Come to Me when you are joyful, and I will share your Joy, multiplying it many times over. I am All you need, just when you need it. Your deepest desires find fulfillment in Me alone.

"This is the age of self-help. Bookstores abound with books about 'taking care of number one,' making oneself the center of all things. The main goal of these methodologies is to become self-sufficient and confident. You, however, have been called to take a 'road less traveled': continual dependence on Me. True confidence comes from knowing you are complete in My Presence. Everything you need has its counterpart in Me."

—From *Jesus Calling*, October 26

5. ***What do you think are the deepest desires that find fulfillment in Jesus alone?***

6. ***Do you long to be self-sufficient and confident on your own, or are you happy to be dependent on Jesus? Explain.***

STUDY IT

Read aloud the following passage from Isaiah 55:1–3, 6–11. This section of Isaiah is commonly referred to as "The Book of Comfort," because it contains many statements in which God reassured His people of His love. At the time, they needed this message because they had been enslaved by foreign powers as a result of their quest to fulfill their longings through idol worship. The Lord was calling them—just as He calls His people in every era—to return to the true Source of fulfillment.

> [1] "Come, all you who are thirsty,
> come to the waters;
> and you who have no money,
> come, buy and eat!
> Come, buy wine and milk
> without money and without cost.
> [2] Why spend money on what is not bread,
> and your labor on what does not satisfy?
> Listen, listen to me, and eat what is good,
> and you will delight in the richest of fare.
> [3] Give ear and come to me;
> listen, that you may live. . . .
> [6] Seek the LORD while he may be found;
> call on him while he is near.

[7] Let the wicked forsake their ways
and the unrighteous their thoughts.
Let them turn to the Lord, and he will have mercy on them,
and to our God, for he will freely pardon.
[8] "For my thoughts are not your thoughts,
neither are your ways my ways,"
declares the Lord.
[9] "As the heavens are higher than the earth,
so are my ways higher than your ways
and my thoughts than your thoughts.
[10] As the rain and the snow
come down from heaven,
and do not return to it
without watering the earth
and making it bud and flourish,
so that it yields seed for the sower and bread for the eater,
[11] so is my word that goes out from my mouth:
It will not return to me empty,
but will accomplish what I desire
and achieve the purpose for which I sent it.

7. ***How would you answer God's question in verse 2: "Why spend money on what is not bread, and your labor on what does not satisfy?" How do people do this? Why do people do this?***

8. ***In verses 2–3, the Lord repeats the words, "Listen, listen to me . . . Give ear . . . listen." Why is listening to Christ so important when it comes to receiving what He has to offer?***

9. ***In verse 8, the Lord says, "For my thoughts are not your thoughts, neither are your ways my ways." Give an example of a human thought or way, and contrast it with the way Jesus thinks about things.***

10. ***What final reason for putting Jesus first is found in verses 10–11?***

11. *Take two minutes of silence to reread the passage, looking for a sentence, phrase, or even one word that stands out as something Jesus may want you to focus on in your life. If you're meeting with a group, the leader will keep track of time. At the end of two minutes, you may share with the group the word or phrase that came to you in the silence.*

12. *Read the passage aloud again. Take another two minutes of silence, prayerfully considering what response God might want you to make to what you have read in His Word. If you're meeting with a group, the leader will again keep track of time. At the end of two minutes, you may share with the group what came to you in the silence if you wish.*

13. *If you're meeting with a group, how can the members pray for you? If you're using this study on your own, what would you like to say to God right now?*

LIVE IT

The theme of this week's daily Scripture readings is seeking Jesus first in your times of longing and spiritual thirst. Read each passage slowly, pausing to think about what is being said. Rather than approaching this as an assignment to complete, think of it as an opportunity to meet with the One who loves you most. Use any of the questions that are helpful.

Day 1

Read Deuteronomy 8:15–18. In this passage, the Israelites are about to enter the Promised Land, and Moses wants them to reflect on the time they spent hungering and thirsting in the wilderness. What were the people supposed to have learned from the experience?

How do you remind yourself that it is the Lord who enables you to produce wealth and everything else? Do you tend to rely on your own power? Why or why not?

Which attitude are you most prone to: that God provides for you abundantly and reliably, or that He doesn't adequately come through for you? Explain.

Spend some time thanking God for giving you the ability to produce what you and your family need.

Day 2

Read Psalm 42:1–3. Does your soul thirst for God as the psalmist describes? If so, what's the evidence? If not, why not?

In your life with the Lord, has anyone (even a voice inside you) ever mockingly said, "Where is your God?" (verse 3). How did that make you feel? How did you respond?

How can you put Jesus first in a situation like the one the psalmist describes?

Spend some time today getting in touch with your inner thirst, which is actually a longing for God. Allow that longing to well up and motivate you to words or action.

Day 3

Read Isaiah 41:17–20. How are the people portrayed in this passage? To what extent can you identify with this description?

How is the Lord portrayed in this passage? How does this compare to the way you have experienced Him?

How do you think this passage is meant to affect what its readers think, feel, and do? What can you do in response to it?

Talk with God about your thirst. Ask Him to help you recognize that it is primarily a longing for Him, and only secondarily a longing for other things.

Day 4

Read John 4:10–15. In the language of Jesus' day, "living water" meant flowing water as opposed to a still pool or lake. What additional meaning might Jesus be conveying when He speaks of living water in verse 10?

What do you think Jesus means when He says, "Whoever drinks the water I give them will never thirst" (verse 14)? How can we make sense of His words, given that even Christians still experience thirst?

What might Jesus mean when He says, "Indeed, the water I give them will become in them a spring of water welling up to eternal life" (verse 14)? Do you have a spring of water welling up inside you? If so, describe your experience.

Thank Jesus for the living water He gives to anyone who asks. If you're not aware of this spring of living water welling up inside you, make a plan to spend time in His presence today.

Day 5

Read John 7:37–39. What did Jesus mean when He said to the crowd, "Let anyone who is thirsty come to me and drink"? How do we follow Jesus' words in our lives today?

What does the Holy Spirit have to do with the living water that Jesus is talking about?

How would you summarize what you've learned about longing and the way to get your thirst quenched? What difference will this make for you today?

Praise Jesus for His offer to permanently satisfy your deepest needs when you choose to follow Him. Look for new ways to put Him first as you go through your day.

SESSION 6

PUTTING JESUS FIRST IN RELATIONSHIPS

Consider It

Many of us have to juggle family and work responsibilities. We may have children, aging parents, and/or siblings to care for. We also have relationships to foster with friends and other loved ones. With all the pressure we're under to fulfill our responsibilities to the people in our lives, it can feel like yet another enormous expectation to put Jesus ahead of all of them.

But the truth is that putting Jesus first helps the other responsibilities fall into place. We worry less. We receive Christ's help in our interactions and service to others. We're less driven to achieve our own ideals of perfection or "the perfect family." We find it easier to extend grace to difficult people, because we understand that God has extended that same grace to us.

There is no doubt that relationships—whether with friends or family members—can be tricky. But as we'll see in this session, putting Jesus first is the key to getting along with people and placing our relationships in the proper perspective.

1. *Describe the basics of your family situation: names and ages of children, siblings, spouse, parents. Which of these individuals, if any, are you actively caring for in some capacity?*

2. *When you were growing up, was Jesus first in your parents' lives? How did Jesus' place in your home—whether He was a priority or not—affect the way they treated you and your siblings?*

Experience It

"Entrust your loved ones to Me; release them into My protective care. They are much safer with Me than in your clinging hands. If you let a loved one become an idol in your heart, you endanger that one—as well as yourself. Joseph and his father, Jacob, suffered terribly because Jacob *loved Joseph more than any of his other sons* and treated him with special favor. So Joseph's brothers hated him and plotted against him. Ultimately, I used that situation for good, but both father and son had to endure years of suffering and separation from one another.

"I detest idolatry, even in the form of parental love, so beware of making a beloved child your idol. When you release loved ones to Me, you are free to cling to My hand. As you entrust others into My care, I am free to shower blessings on them. *My Presence will go with them wherever they go, and I will give them rest.* This same Presence stays with you as you relax and place your trust in Me. Watch to see what I will do."

—From *Jesus Calling*, August 23

3. ***What are some signs that a loved one might be an idol in a person's life?***

4. ***What would be some reasons for entrusting loved ones to Jesus' care? How can we be sure we've done this?***

"*You cannot serve two masters.* If I am truly your Master, you will desire to please Me above all others. If pleasing people is your goal, you will be enslaved to them. People can be harsh taskmasters when you give them this power over you.

"If I am the Master of your life, I will also be your *First Love*. Your serving Me is rooted and grounded in My vast, unconditional Love for you. The lower you bow down before Me, the higher I lift you up into intimate relationship with Me. *The Joy of living in My Presence* outshines all other pleasures. I want you to reflect My joyous Light by living in increasing intimacy with Me."

—FROM *JESUS CALLING*, MAY 3

5. ***What are some ways you can show that God is the First Love in your life?***

6. ***How can treating Jesus as the Master of your life affect the way you relate to others?***

Study It

Read aloud the following passage from Genesis 37:2–7, 17–28. These verses tell the story of a man named Jacob (his other name was Israel) and eleven of his sons. Jacob had two wives and two concubines. Joseph was the son of his favorite wife, Rachel, who had died giving birth to Benjamin, the youngest son in the family (not mentioned in this passage). Reuben was the oldest of Jacob's sons. Note that the ornate robe given to Joseph would have signified to his brothers that he was Jacob's choice to lead the clan—an honor normally bestowed on the firstborn son.

> [2] Joseph, a young man of seventeen, was tending the flocks with his brothers, the sons of Bilhah and the sons of Zilpah, his father's wives, and he brought their father a bad report about them.
>
> [3] Now Israel loved Joseph more than any of his other sons, because he had been born to him in his old age; and he made an ornate robe for him. [4] When his brothers saw that their father loved him more than any of them, they hated him and could not speak a kind word to him.
>
> [5] Joseph had a dream, and when he told it to his brothers, they hated him all the more. [6] He said to them, "Listen to this dream I had: [7] We were binding sheaves of grain out in the field when suddenly my sheaf rose and stood upright, while your sheaves gathered around mine and bowed down to it." . . .
>
> [17] So Joseph went after his brothers and found them near Dothan. [18] But they saw him in the distance, and before he reached them, they plotted to kill him.
>
> [19] "Here comes that dreamer!" they said to each other. [20] "Come now, let's kill him and throw him into one of these cisterns and say that a ferocious animal devoured him. Then we'll see what comes of his dreams."
>
> [21] When Reuben heard this, he tried to rescue him from their hands. "Let's not take his life," he said. [22] "Don't shed any blood. Throw him into

this cistern here in the wilderness, but don't lay a hand on him." Reuben said this to rescue him from them and take him back to his father.

[23] So when Joseph came to his brothers, they stripped him of his robe—the ornate robe he was wearing—[24] and they took him and threw him into the cistern. The cistern was empty; there was no water in it.

[25]As they sat down to eat their meal, they looked up and saw a caravan of Ishmaelites coming from Gilead. Their camels were loaded with spices, balm and myrrh, and they were on their way to take them down to Egypt.

[26] Judah said to his brothers, "What will we gain if we kill our brother and cover up his blood? [27]Come, let's sell him to the Ishmaelites and not lay our hands on him; after all, he is our brother, our own flesh and blood." His brothers agreed.

[28] So when the Midianite merchants came by, his brothers pulled Joseph up out of the cistern and sold him for twenty shekels of silver to the Ishmaelites, who took him to Egypt.

7. ***What did Jacob/Israel do that created problems within the family?***

8. ***What did Joseph do that wasn't wise?***

9. ***What did Joseph's brothers discuss doing to him because of their jealousy? What did they end up doing? Do you find these reactions to be surprising? Why or why not?***

10. ***Have you ever treated one of your children better than the others, or unlovingly put your children ahead of your spouse, or put any family member ahead of Jesus? If so, what happened? If not, how have you avoided it?***

11. ***Take two minutes of silence to reread the passage, looking for a sentence, phrase, or even one word that stands out as something Jesus may want you to focus on in your life. If you're meeting with a group, the leader will keep track of time. At the end of two minutes, you may share with the group the word or phrase that came to you in the silence.***

12. ***Read the passage aloud again. Take another two minutes of silence, prayerfully considering what response God might want you to make to what you have read in His Word. If you're meeting with a group, the leader will again keep track of time. At the end of two minutes, you may share with the group what came to you in the silence if you wish.***

13. ***If you're meeting with a group, how can the members pray for you? If you're using this study on your own, what would you like to say to God right now?***

Live It

The theme of this week's daily Scripture readings, which continues the story of Joseph and his brothers, centers on putting Jesus first in your relationships with your family and with others whom God brings into your life. Read each passage slowly, pausing to think about what is being said. Rather than approaching this as an assignment to complete, think of it as an opportunity to meet with the One who loves you most. Use any of the questions that are helpful.

Day 1

Read Genesis 37:29–35. How did Jacob suffer for the favoritism he showed to Joseph?

Jacob "refused to be comforted" after the death of Joseph (verse 35). What might it have looked like in Jacob's life to put God first in his family after this loss?

What opportunity do you have today to put God first in your family and your life?

Thank God today for His mercy in the way He deals with you and your family.

Day 2

Read Genesis 39:1–20. How did God show mercy to Joseph?

What are the signs that Joseph was putting God first when it came to honoring his master?

What steps did Joseph take in his interactions with Potiphar's wife to ensure that he would not sin against God? What was the result of his decision?

Praise God for giving you the strength to do what He has called you to do once you have devoted yourself to Him.

Day 3

Read Genesis 39:20–40:23. How did God bless Joseph even though he was now in prison?

How did Joseph interpret the dream of the chief cupbearer? What hopes did he place in this man?

Even though the Lord was with Joseph, difficult things still happened to him in his journey. People still disappointed him and dashed his hopes. How can you be sure the Lord is with you in your journey as a Christian, even when similar hard things happen to you?

If you're a child of God, look for signs that Jesus is with you today. Thank Him for His presence.

Day 4

Read Genesis 41:1–40. Joseph had asked the chief cupbearer to remember him once the man was restored to Pharaoh's household, but the cupbearer had forgotten him. What situation ultimately caused the cupbearer to remember Joseph?

How did God give favor to Joseph in his meeting with Pharaoh? What might have happened if Joseph had lost patience and given up on keeping God first in his life?

How did Joseph's faithfulness to God lead to not only blessing for himself but for the entire region of Egypt and Canaan?

Make a deliberate decision to put your relationships in God's hands today. Ask Him to help you through the times of waiting when it seems that no progress is being made.

Day 5

Read Genesis 42:1–17 and 45:1–13. How did Joseph put God first in his relationship with his brothers when they came to Egypt to buy food?

Why do you think Joseph called them spies and told them to bring his younger brother, Benjamin, to him? What change was he hoping to see in them?

At the end of the story, Joseph reconciles with his brothers. How did keeping God first allow him to see the bigger picture of what God was doing in the family as a whole?

Praise Jesus for His offer to be with you and your family, regardless of the circumstances you're facing. Ask Him to show you the big picture of how He can work in your life as a believer.

SESSION 7

Putting Jesus First in Finances

Consider It

When you look at Jesus' teachings in the Gospels, you come to a startling conclusion: *Jesus talked about people's relationship with money more than almost any other topic.* Of the many parables in the Gospels (most experts say there are about forty), an overwhelming number of these either directly speak about money (such as the parable of the pearl of great price in Matthew 13:45–46), or they touch on material wealth (such as the parable of the rich man and Lazarus in Luke 16:19–31).

Why did Jesus talk so frequently about money? His statement in Matthew 6:24 sheds some light on the issue: "You cannot serve both God and money." In the original Greek, the word translated as "money" is *mammon.* This ancient word refers less to coins or cash than it does to people's feelings about their wealth—their pursuit of it as a top priority in their lives. Just as the book of Proverbs personified Wisdom as a positive force (see 1:21–33), the Gospel writers personified Mammon as a negative force, much like a false god that people worship.

The way we spend our money reveals a great deal about our priorities. It also reveals a great deal about whom we choose to serve. This week, we will look at the importance of putting Jesus first when it comes to our finances.

1. ***What is one word that comes to mind when you think of money?***

2. ***What role does money play in your life? What role would you like it to play?***

Experience It

"When something in your life or thoughts makes you anxious, come to Me and talk about it. Bring Me your *prayer and petition with thanksgiving*, saying, 'Thank You, Jesus, for this opportunity to trust You more.' Though the lessons of trust that I send to you come wrapped in difficulties, the benefits far outweigh the cost.

"Well-developed trust will bring you many blessings, not the least of which is My Peace. I have promised to *keep you in perfect Peace* to the extent that you trust in Me. The world has it backward, teaching that peace is the result of having enough money, possessions, insurance, and security systems. *My* Peace, however, is such an all-encompassing gift that it is independent of all circumstances. Though you lose everything else, if you gain My Peace you are rich indeed."

—From *Jesus Calling*, March 1

3. ***How do you respond to the idea of taking your money issues to Jesus and saying, "Thank You for this opportunity to trust You more"? How would this compare to the way you usually act?***

4. ***Why is money an unreliable source of peace?***

"When some basic need is lacking—time, energy, money—consider yourself blessed. Your very lack is an opportunity to latch onto Me in unashamed dependence. When you begin a day with inadequate resources, you must concentrate your efforts on the present moment. This is where you are meant to live—in the present. It is the place where I always await you. Awareness of your inadequacy is a rich blessing, training you to rely wholeheartedly on Me.

"The truth is that self-sufficiency is a myth perpetuated by pride and temporary success. Health and wealth can disappear instantly, as can life itself. Rejoice in your insufficiency, knowing that *My Power is made perfect in weakness*."

—From *Jesus Calling*, April 30

5. ***Think about how you should live if you lack money. How easy or difficult is it for you to live that way?***

6. ***Have you ever had temporary success go away unexpectedly? How did the experience affect you and your sense of self-sufficiency?***

STUDY IT

Read aloud the following passage from Haggai 1:2–11. The prophet Haggai lived in a fragile time for the Jewish people. In 586 BC, the Babylonians destroyed Judah (and its capital, Jerusalem), reduced the temple to rubble, and carried most of the Jews off to exile. Decades later, in 538 BC, the Persians defeated the Babylonians, and King Cyrus gave the Jews permission to go home and rebuild Jerusalem. The people started well, but problems hindered them from finishing the job. They got caught up in just making a living and resisting the opposition of enemies, and thus, fifteen years went by with no work on the temple. Finally, in 520 BC, Haggai spoke to them about getting back to the priority of building a place to worship the Lord.

> [2] This is what the LORD Almighty says: "These people say, 'The time has not yet come to rebuild the LORD's house.'"
>
> [3] Then the word of the LORD came through the prophet Haggai: [4] "Is it a time for you yourselves to be living in your paneled houses, while this house remains a ruin?"
>
> [5] Now this is what the LORD Almighty says: "Give careful thought to your ways. [6] You have planted much, but harvested little. You eat, but never have enough. You drink, but never have your fill. You put on clothes, but are not warm. You earn wages, only to put them in a purse with holes in it."

[7] This is what the Lord Almighty says: "Give careful thought to your ways. [8] Go up into the mountains and bring down timber and build my house, so that I may take pleasure in it and be honored," says the Lord. [9] "You expected much, but see, it turned out to be little. What you brought home, I blew away. Why?" declares the Lord Almighty. "Because of my house, which remains a ruin, while each of you is busy with your own house. [10] Therefore, because of you the heavens have withheld their dew and the earth its crops. [11] I called for a drought on the fields and the mountains, on the grain, the new wine, the olive oil and everything else the ground produces, on people and livestock, and on all the labor of your hands."

7. ***What does this passage indicate about the economic conditions the Jews were experiencing?***

8. ***In such economic times, the people were inclined to focus all the more on their own needs. Why was this a mistake?***

9. *How is your situation similar to the situation the Israelites were facing?*

10. *What does putting Jesus first in our finances look like other than giving money to support His work in the world?*

11. *Take two minutes of silence to reread the passage, looking for a sentence, phrase, or even one word that stands out as something Jesus may want you to focus on in your life. If you're meeting with a group, the leader will keep track of time. At the end of two minutes, you may share with the group the word or phrase that came to you in the silence.*

12. ***Read the passage aloud again. Take another two minutes of silence, prayerfully considering what response God might want you to make to what you have read in His Word. If you're meeting with a group, the leader will again keep track of time. At the end of two minutes, you may share with the group what came to you in the silence if you wish.***

13. ***If you're meeting with a group, how can the members pray for you? If you're using this study on your own, what would you like to say to God right now?***

Live It

The theme of this week's daily Scripture readings is on putting Jesus first in your finances—and recognizing that everything you have comes from your heavenly Father. Read each passage slowly, pausing to think about what is being said. Rather than approaching this as an assignment to complete, think of it as an opportunity to meet with the One who loves you most. Use any of the questions that are helpful.

Day 1

Read Matthew 6:19–24. What does Jesus mean when He says you are to "store up for yourselves treasures in heaven" (verse 20)? How is this accomplished?

Why does money (Mammon) so easily become a master or god in our lives (see verse 24)? Why can't we serve both Jesus and money?

What step can you take today to dethrone money as a ruling power in your life?

Today, ask Jesus to help you love Him more than money. Be honest with Him about the power that money has in your life.

Day 2

Read Matthew 26:6–13. What did the woman do with the expensive perfumed oil (which was probably one of her family's prized possessions)? Why did she do it?

What did Jesus' disciples want the woman to do with the perfumed oil (see verses 8–9)? How sensible do you think their view was? Why?

How easy is it for you to be extravagant in what you give to Jesus? Why is that the case?

Give your heart and your full attention to Jesus in prayer today. Ask Him how you can worship Him through your resources.

Day 3

Read 1 Timothy 6:9–11. What is wrong with the desire to get rich?

Paul warns against the love of money, not money itself, as the root of many kinds of evil. How can you tell if you have this type of love of money?

What antidote to the love of money does Paul recommend in verse 11? Why is this good advice?

Tell Jesus that you want to pursue righteousness, godliness, faith, love, endurance, and gentleness today. Look for steps you can take in that pursuit.

Day 4

Read Hebrews 13:5–6. What reason does the writer give Christians for being content with what they have?

The writer speaks in verse 6 about fear. What are some ways that fear can lead to the love of money?

Is the love of money or fear about money a problem for you? If so, how? How can you address that love or fear so that it doesn't control your thoughts, words, or actions?

Talk with Jesus about your love of money or your fears regarding it. Tell Him honestly how it affects you, and ask Him to release the control that it has in your life.

Day 5

Read James 4:13–17. What is James against here? Is it making plans, or something else?

How does James instruct you to put Jesus first in your life?

In what ways have you been guilty of "boasting" about the future? How would taking the stance of "if it is the Lord's will" improve the way you think about your plans and projects?

Open up to Jesus about what you've learned about your attitude toward money this past week. Ask Him to give you deeper humility, great confidence in Him, and a richer awareness of His presence as you make ongoing decisions about money.

SESSION 8

Putting Jesus First and Serving Him Alone

Consider It

During this study, we've looked at ways the Bible instructs us to put Jesus first with our schedules, our anxieties and fears, our plans for the future, our longings, and our finances and relationships. All of this comes down to one central truth: *God calls us to put Him first in everything we do.* He calls us to trust in Him alone as the only One who can truly meet our needs—both physical and spiritual. When we put other things first in our lives, we tend to serve those things and treat them as gods.

In the Bible, this was a huge problem for God's people, the Israelites. The Lord had commanded them to have no other gods before Him (see Exodus 20:3), but again and again the people turned to idol worship. Even though today we're not tempted to worship religious images of wood and stone as they were, we still have an ever-present temptation to turn to things other than God to meet our needs. An *idol* can be defined as anything we love more than Jesus, or anything we put ahead of Jesus in our order of priorities. Status and power, security and control, money and material comforts, work and achievement, binge eating and starving ourselves—all these and more can become idols for us.

Jesus wants to dethrone the idols in our lives. He wants to be our First Love. In this session, we'll consider the allure of idols, identify some things we're tempted to idolize, and look at what the Bible says we can do to overcome these temptations.

1. ***What are some pursuits that people in the world put ahead of Jesus today? Why do people devote themselves to such idols?***

2. ***What is one thing in your life that you're prone to treat as an idol? What are you tempted to love more than Jesus or serve more than Jesus?***

Experience It

"Worship Me only. Whatever occupies your mind the most becomes your god. Worries, if indulged, develop into idols. Anxiety gains a life of its own, parasitically infesting your mind. Break free from this bondage by affirming your trust in Me and refreshing yourself in My Presence. What goes on in your mind is invisible, undetectable to other people. But I read your thoughts continually, searching for evidence of trust in Me. I rejoice when your mind turns toward Me. Guard your thoughts diligently; good thought-choices will keep you close to Me."

—From *Jesus Calling*, January 30

3. ***What occupies your mind the most? Has this been the case for a long time, or has this person or thing dominated your thoughts only for a season?***

4. ***How should you shake off the bondage of an idol? Have you ever successfully done this? If so, how did doing it affect you?***

"Save your best striving for seeking My Face. I am constantly communicating with you. To find Me and hear My voice, you must seek Me above all else. Anything that you desire more than Me becomes an idol. When you are determined to get your own way, you blot Me out of your consciousness. Instead of single-mindedly pursuing some goal, talk with Me about it. Let the Light of My Presence shine on this pursuit so that you can see it from My perspective. If the goal fits into My plans for you, I will help you reach it. If it is contrary to My will for you, I will gradually change the desire of your heart. *Seek Me first* and foremost; then the rest of your life will fall into place, piece by piece."

—From *Jesus Calling*, March 8

5. ***How can you tell if you are single-mindedly pursuing a goal in an idolatrous way, as opposed to just staying focused on something important?***

6. ***What is something that you desire right now? Have you talked with Jesus about it? If so, what do you think He has been saying about it?***

Study It

Read aloud the following passage from Isaiah 30:19–26. Isaiah had been warning the people that the Assyrians were going to attack because the Israelites had turned to idols for their needs rather than seeking the Lord. In these verses, the prophet now steps aside from the rebuke and foretells what will happen when they change their ways and decide to put God first. Note that the word *Zion* is another name for Jerusalem, the capital city of the nation.

> [19] People of Zion, who live in Jerusalem, you will weep no more. How gracious he will be when you cry for help! As soon as he hears, he will answer you. [20] Although the Lord gives you the bread of adversity and the water of affliction, your teachers will be hidden no more; with your own eyes you will see them. [21] Whether you turn to the right or to the left, your ears will hear a voice behind you, saying, "This is the way; walk in it." [22] Then you will desecrate your idols overlaid with silver and your images covered with gold; you will throw them away like a menstrual cloth and say to them, "Away with you!"
>
> [23] He will also send you rain for the seed you sow in the ground, and the food that comes from the land will be rich and plentiful. In that day your cattle will graze in broad meadows. [24] The oxen and donkeys that work the soil will eat fodder and mash, spread out with fork and shovel. [25] In the day of great slaughter, when the towers fall, streams of

water will flow on every high mountain and every lofty hill. [26] The moon will shine like the sun, and the sunlight will be seven times brighter, like the light of seven full days, when the Lord binds up the bruises of his people and heals the wounds he inflicted.

7. *What assurances were the people given in verses 19–21 if they chose to honor God?*

8. *Are there areas in your life that you feel you need to clearly hear from God about whether or not to pursue? If so, what are those areas?*

9. *What are some things God promises to the redeemed in verses 23–26? How are these like the blessings you hope for when you throw away your idols and decide to put Jesus first?*

10. ***Why is it more challenging to throw away our idols when the Lord gives us "the bread of adversity and the water of affliction" (verse 20)?***

11. ***Take two minutes of silence to reread the passage, looking for a sentence, phrase, or even one word that stands out as something Jesus may want you to focus on in your life. If you're meeting with a group, the leader will keep track of time. At the end of two minutes, you may share with the group the word or phrase that came to you in the silence.***

12. ***Read the passage aloud again. Take another two minutes of silence, prayerfully considering what response God might want you to make to what you have read in His Word. If you're meeting with a group, the leader will again keep track of time. At the end of two minutes, you may share with the group what came to you in the silence if you wish.***

13. ***If you're meeting with a group, how can the members pray for you? If you're using this study on your own, what would you like to say to God right now?***

Live It

The theme of this week's daily Scripture readings is trusting only in Jesus to provide for your needs. Read each passage slowly, pausing to think about what is being said. Rather than approaching this as an assignment to complete, think of it as an opportunity to meet with the One who loves you most. Use any of the questions that are helpful.

Day 1

Read Exodus 32:1–6. These events took place just after the Lord had freed the Israelites from slavery in Egypt, rescued them from the Egyptians, and led them to Mount Sinai for further instructions. Given all He'd done, why did the people want an idol at a moment like this?

What was the appeal of a gold statue in the shape of a calf? Why would they worship it? (Consider the effect that having grown up in Egypt might have had on their thinking.)

What is so appealing about the gods our culture turns to in times of distress?

Ask Jesus today for strength to resist the gods of our culture. Confess the appeal they have for you, and seek His help in saying no to them in concrete ways.

Day 2

Read Exodus 32:7–14. How did the Lord respond when the people had a party to celebrate their new idol?

Why do you think the Lord responded like this?

How did Moses persuade the Lord not to destroy His people? What does Moses' approach tell you about the God we serve?

Let your prayers today be shaped by an awareness of how important it is to worship the Lord alone. Tell Him why He deserves your complete loyalty.

Day 3

Read Exodus 32:25–35. How did Moses address the problem of idolatry? How did the Lord address it?

Why is idolatry so serious?

How will reading about this episode with the golden calf affect your attitude about the things or people you are tempted to idolize?

Watch for ways to put the Lord first in your life today. Be on the lookout for anything that threatens to get in the way.

Day 4

Read Deuteronomy 7:1–6. Why did the Lord forbid His people to intermarry with the pagan groups who occupied the Promised Land when the Israelites first arrived? What was the wisdom of this?

Have you ever known a person to be spiritually led astray by a spouse or other partner? Why is it so easy for this to happen?

Christians are not called to kill off the people whose lifestyles tempt them to go astray. Instead, how does the Lord want us to relate to them?

Tune in to how you are *tempted* by the culture around you—which is different from how you may be *offended* by the culture. Notice the subtle ways you are inclined to join in what others think and do. Ask the Lord to open your eyes.

Day 5

Read Deuteronomy 7:7–11. Why did God say He set His affection on the Israelites?

What motivations does this passage give every Christian for obeying the Lord?

What can we learn about the Lord from this passage?

Ask the Lord today to help you respond to His love with loyalty and by putting Him first in everything you do.

LEADER'S NOTES

Thank you for your willingness to lead a group through this *Jesus Calling* study. The rewards of leading are different from the rewards of participating, and we hope you find your own walk with Jesus deepened by this experience. In many ways, your group meeting will be structured like other Bible studies in which you've participated. You'll want to open in prayer, for example, and ask people to silence their phones. These leader's notes will focus on elements of the study that may be new to you.

Consider It

This first portion of the study functions as an icebreaker. It gets the group members thinking about the topic at hand by asking them to share things from their own experience. Some people may be tempted to tell a long story in response to one of these questions, but the goal is to keep the answers brief. Ideally, you want everyone in the group to have a chance to answer the *Consider It* questions, so you may want to say up front that everyone needs to limit his or her answer to one minute.

With the rest of the study, it is generally not a good idea to go around the circle and have everyone answer every question—a free-flowing discussion is more desirable. But with the *Consider It* questions, you can go around the circle. Encourage shy people to share, but don't force them. Tell the group they should feel free to pass if they prefer not to answer a question.

Experience It

This is the group's chance to talk about excerpts from the *Jesus Calling* devotional. You will need to monitor this discussion closely so that you have enough time for the actual study of God's Word that follows. If the group has a long and rich discussion on one of the devotional excerpts, you may choose to skip the other one and move on to the Bible study. Don't feel obliged to cover every *Experience It* question if the conversation is fruitful. On the other hand, do move on if the group gets off on a tangent.

Study It

Try to do the *Study It* exercise in session 1 on your own before the group meets the first time so you can coach people on what to expect. Note that this section may be a little different from Bible studies your group has done in the past. The group will talk about the Bible passage as usual, but then there will be several minutes of silence so individuals can pray about what God might want to say to them personally through the reading. It will be up to you to keep track of the time and call people back to the discussion when the time is up. (There are some good timer apps that play a gentle chime or other pleasant sound instead of a disruptive noise.) If the group members aren't used to being silent in a group, brief them on what to expect.

Don't be afraid to let people sit in silence. Two minutes of quiet may seem like a long time at first, but it will help to train group members to sit in silence with God when they are alone. They can remain where they are in the circle, or if you have space, you can let them go off by themselves to other rooms at your instruction. If your group meets in a home, ask the host before the meeting which rooms are available for use. Some people will be more comfortable in the quiet if they have a bit of space from others.

When the group reconvenes after the time of silence, invite them to share what they experienced. There are several questions provided in this study guide that you can ask. Note that it's not necessary to cover every question if the group has a good discussion going. It's also not necessary to go around the circle and make everyone share.

Don't be concerned if the group members are reserved and slow to share after the exercise. People are often quiet when they are pulling together their ideas, and the exercise will have been a new experience for many of them. Just ask a question and let it hang in the air until someone speaks up. You can then say, "Thank you. What about others? What came to you when you sat with the passage?"

Some people may say they found it hard to quiet their minds enough to focus on the passage for those few minutes. Tell them this is okay. They are practicing a skill, and sometimes skills take time to learn. If they learn to sit quietly with God's Word in a group, they will become much more comfortable sitting with the Word on their own. Remind them that spending time in the Bible each day is one of the most valuable things they can do as believers in Christ.

Preparation

It's not necessary for group members to prepare anything for the study ahead of time. However, at the end of each study are five days' worth of suggestions for spending time in God's Word during the next week. These daily times are optional but valuable, so encourage the group to do them. Also, invite them to bring their questions and insights to the group at your next meeting, especially if they had a breakthrough moment or if they didn't understand something.

As the leader, there are a few things you should do to prepare for each meeting:

- *Read through the session.* This will help you become familiar with the content and know how to structure the discussion times.

- *Spend five to ten minutes doing the* Study It *questions on your own.* When the group meets, you'll be watching the clock, so you'll probably have a more fulfilling time with the passage if you do the exercise ahead of time. You can then spend time in the passage again with the group. This way, you'll be sure to have the key verses for that session deeply in your mind.

- *Pray for your group.* Pray especially that God will guide them into a deeper understanding of how they can learn to continually dwell in His peace.

- *Bring extra supplies to your meeting.* Group members should bring their own pens for writing notes on the Bible reflection, but it is a good idea to have extras available for those who forget. You may also want to bring paper and Bibles for those who may have neglected to bring their study guides to the meeting.

Below you will find suggested answers for some of the study questions. Note that in many cases there is no one right answer, especially when the group members are sharing their personal experiences.

Session 1: Putting Jesus First in Times of Busyness

1. *Answers will vary, but it's likely the group members will feel stressed to some degree by the amount of things they have on their plates. Urge them to keep their responses to about a minute. Our society tends to consider busyness as a badge of honor and a symbol of importance, so don't allow the group members to reinforce this idea by going on too long about their hectic lives!*

2. *We place value on it, in part, because we value productivity. We tend to think of people like machines—and a good machine is a productive machine. This becomes a problem when we seek to put Jesus first, because He wants us to put His kingdom and His work above our own goals (see Matthew 6:33).*

3. *Recognizing Jesus as our boss includes allowing Him to set the priorities on our agenda—letting Him choose what is essential for us to accomplish and what is less important, regardless of what the world thinks. It also involves allowing Jesus to decide the way in which we work and letting Him choose the place where we will do our work.*

4. *When our plans are thwarted, it helps to be on the lookout for Christ's work in our lives. When things are going according to our own plans, it's easy for us as believers to lose sight of God's presence and the bigger picture of what He is doing within us. Treating disruptions as divine interventions allows us to focus on God's agenda rather than our own and put Him first.*

5. *Making time to be still in Jesus' presence is important because it turns our attention to the things that truly matter to Him—and keeps us from missing out on the richness of what He has planned for His followers. Even a two-minute pause to put Jesus first in the midst of a hectic day can help us to stay on track with Him.*

6. *One sign that we are seeking Christ primarily for His gifts is when we take the time to make prayer requests but don't take the time to worship Him or* *to sit quietly in His Presence and submit our thoughts to Him. This is tragic, because He is worth infinitely more than anything He gives us.*

7. *Martha thought putting Jesus first meant working hard to meet His needs for food and shelter when He came to visit. She put aside all her other responsibilities—whatever they might have been—to show hospitality to Jesus and His disciples. Given her culture, this was an accepted way of putting someone first, and even today, it is important to serve others in love. However, as followers of Christ, we need to always put Him first, spending time in His presence each day so we can receive what He has to teach us.*

8. *Mary thought putting Jesus first meant sitting at His feet like a disciple, listening to His teaching. She put aside all her normal tasks—whatever they might have been—to stop and listen to Him. This is something we also need to do each day, since Jesus praises it as the better choice. While we may not always be able to spend the whole day sitting in Jesus' presence, we can certainly carve out some "Mary time" in a "Martha day."*

9. *The point of this account is not that we should completely abandon our daily work, but that we should put our view of work in proper perspective. Achieving results—regardless of how noble our goals might be—is not of ultimate importance to the Lord. Rather, He wants us to spend time in fellowship with Him each day, sitting at His feet and just being in His presence. This needs to be a priority in our day, even as we tend to other essential tasks such as taking care of matters at work and with our families.*

10. *Answers will vary. As the leader, be open about your own habits and how you try to carve out time to be with Jesus in the midst of a full day. Maybe you spend a chunk of time with Him in the morning and then check in with Him briefly throughout the day. Or maybe you set aside a block of time at noon to get away from distractions, pray, and read God's Word. Also share some ways you've learned to listen less to the "voices" in your world that tempt you to put other things ahead of Christ.*

11. *Answers will vary. It's fine for this process to be unfamiliar to the group at first. Be sure to keep track of time.*

12. *Answers will vary. Note that some people may find the silence intimidating at first. Their anxiety might tempt them to fill the air with noise, but it will be helpful for these group members to just take a quiet moment before God. Let them express their discomfort once you're all gathered together again, but make sure it is balanced by those who found the silence strengthening. Helping people become comfortable with this "holy quiet" will serve their private daily times with God in wonderful ways.*

13. *Take as much time as you can to pray for each other. You might have someone write down the prayer requests so you can keep track of answers to prayer.*

Session 2: Putting Jesus First in Times of Anxiety

1. *Answers will vary. The tendency to worry seems to be hardwired into us at a young age. Some of us are just naturally less prone to worry, though—and while that's a good thing, it's a gift rather than an accomplishment. Those of us who are natural worriers, however, need to seek Jesus to overcome this ingrained tendency.*

2. *We falsely believe that, by worrying, we have some control over uncontrollable events. Our worrying over time becomes a habit—we don't do it for rational reasons but because we've conditioned our minds to go down these pathways. That's why we need to train our minds to return to Jesus and focus on Him in times of stress.*

3. *The first step in displacing worry is to choose to spend time with Jesus. As His followers, we can talk with Him about the things we're worried about and honestly express our feelings to Him, understanding that He knows our needs and will take care of them. We can simply bask in His Presence in silence and solitude.*

4. *When we, as Christians, seek Jesus, He will shower His perfect peace into the pool of our minds. He will bless our lives and shine His light into every situation we face. Be ready to share your experience of this "shower of peace," or His clarifying light and blessings. It will encourage your group members to try setting aside more time to seek Jesus.*

5. *If we are believers in Christ, we don't need to worry because we know we are on the path that God has chosen for us. Although our present circumstances may seem random, we can rest assured that God is directing our steps and has everything under control. Choosing to walk where He leads and trusting in His guidance leads us to a place of peace.*

6. *Ask everyone in the group to answer this question, as it is important for them to consider where they tend to focus their minds. Share your own struggles with rehearsing the past or worrying about the future. And talk about your own efforts to live in the present with Jesus, explaining what you do to lasso your thoughts and bring them back to Christ.*

7. *Jesus states that the people of God don't need to worry because our heavenly Father knows what we need and is willing and able to provide those things to us. He values us far more than the birds and flowers—and if He takes such great care of them, will He not take even greater care of us? The primary issues at stake are whether God cares about us and whether He is active in the lives of His sons and daughters—and in both cases, Jesus' answer is yes. Jesus also says worry is pointless because it accomplishes nothing. It can't lengthen our lives by a single hour.*

8. *Seeking God's kingdom first means putting God's will above our own. It means making obedience to God's Word our top priority in life, doing the right things with the right motives (see Matthew 6:1–18), and staying in fellowship with Christ. Seeking God's kingdom isn't a matter of looking for something that is hidden or absent. The kingdom is present in the lives of* *believers—on earth and in heaven—because the Holy Spirit is present within them (see 1 Corinthians 3:16).*

9. *Some kingdom activities that indicate we are putting Jesus first include showing love to our enemies and praying for those who are hostile to us because of our faith. Other examples could include providing food to the hungry, giving drink to the thirsty, offering hospitality to strangers, clothing those without clothes, helping the sick, and visiting those in prison. We don't "earn" our salvation by doing these things, but by them we do express our gratitude to God for salvation.*

10. *Answers will vary, but putting Jesus ahead of our worries always involves believing that He is in control of our situation, that He cares deeply for us, that He is willing to intervene in our lives, and that He is able to provide for our every need.*

11. *Answers will vary.*

12. *Answers will vary.*

13. *Responses will vary.*

Session 3: Putting Jesus First in Times of Fear

1. *Some group members may find it hard to think of themselves as under threat. Some may worry a lot about terrorism, while others may see that as distant and unlikely to affect them personally. Other members may be particularly aware of Satan's malice toward them. It's fine if some individuals claim to feel fairly safe. If they are believers, they may have already internalized the safety they have in Jesus.*

2. *People tend to handle their fears in different ways. Some take time out to think through the situation and work out a solution. Some people naturally* *tend to face their concerns head on, while others are inclined to run away and seek escape from them. Some people find comfort by talking about their fears. Hopefully, many in the group will choose to confront their fears as David and the psalmists often did—by taking those concerns to God in prayer.*

3. *Gazing at our circumstances tends to make us dizzy or confused because it warps our perspective, causing us to think that what we're facing is greater than Jesus can handle. This can lead Christians to fear, no longer sure of whether we can rely on Jesus to deal with the problems in our lives.*

4. *The key to making Jesus the focal point of our day is to build a habit of returning our minds to Christ throughout the day. To build this habit, we can set an electronic reminder to check in hourly, and then take a moment to rehearse a verse of Scripture such as "Be still, and know that I am God" (Psalm 46:10), or a short prayer such as, "Thank You, Jesus, for . . . ," or "I trust You in this, Jesus." Continually refocusing like this takes only seconds. It's just a means of reminding ourselves to put our circumstances in perspective.*

5. *Answers will vary. Allow a time of silence for people to think about this, as they may not immediately be aware of fears that are surrounding them, or they may not want to be the first to admit them. If no one else wants to speak first, you can share one of your own potential worries. This doesn't have to be something you're obsessing about, just something you could obsess about if you allowed yourself to do so.*

6. *We're more likely to put Jesus first if we trust Him to run our world with wisdom and love. Thankfulness is the habit of noticing what is good in our lives. It feeds trust. Just making the effort to be thankful instead of resentful or anxious is a way of putting Jesus ahead of our natural emotions.*

7. *The psalmist asks the Lord to protect him from shame. He asks to be rescued and delivered from his enemies, who are wicked and cruel. He asks* *for God to be his rock of refuge—the place where he goes for safety. He asks God to continue to take care of him when he is old, just as the Lord did when he was young.*

8. *The psalmist is confident that God will come through for him because he has years of experience with God delivering him. Give the Christians in your group time to think back over their years of knowing Jesus and review how He has cared for them. If they are new to the faith, they can benefit from others' experiences of God's watchfulness over them. And they may then be able to recognize God's hand in their lives even before they knew it was Him.*

9. *Jesus is the only One who can and will deliver! If we seek our hope in other people, we will quickly be disappointed. If our hope is in receiving good things from life because we "deserve" them, we will also be let down. But if, as Christians, we place our hope in the things Jesus has promised, we won't be disappointed. He doesn't necessarily give us everything we want in this life, because not everything we want is a godly desire. But He promises to come through for us on the things that He says are important.*

10. *The psalmist was talking about the great things God did that are recorded in the Old Testament, such as delivering the Israelites from slavery in Egypt, giving them the land of Canaan, and enabling them to defeat the Philistines during the time of David. During times of fear and trial, it is important to remember God's previous acts of deliverance so that we, His people, can remember that He is willing and able to deliver us in the present.*

11. *Answers will vary.*

12. *Answers will vary.*

13. *Responses will vary.*

Session 4: Putting Jesus First in Times of Uncertainty

1. *We all need wisdom about something. In fact, the reality is that we desperately need wisdom for all the decisions we face. We may think we have certain things figured out, but if we knew how much we don't know (even as Christians!), we would be far more dependent on Jesus' guidance and far more willing to say, "Okay, Lord, I'm not in charge. You are."*

2. *Answers will vary. Hopefully, the group members have developed (or are in the process of developing) a daily habit of prayer and seeking God in His Word. Share an example from your own life of how developing such daily habits in times of calm has enabled you to understand God's direction in the more chaotic times. Also, share how God has guided you in some of the big decisions of life, and where His path ultimately led you.*

3. *While there is certainly nothing wrong with setting goals and taking the necessary steps to get there, we need to make sure that we are always involving God in the process first and foremost. Hypervigilant scanning and planning generally reflect a belief that "Life is dangerous; I need to be in control at all times." We forget to trust Jesus and His agenda during these uncertain times. If we really trust Him, we can rely on Him to guide us to the next thing that needs to be done. We will also be able to set our plans aside when He brings us something that He thinks is more important.*

4. *For many of us, trusting in Jesus for the next step doesn't come naturally. There are plan-ahead personalities and don't-plan-ahead personalities, and each has its strengths and weaknesses. However, we must realize that God may not always choose to reveal His long-range plans for His children. He may instead choose to help us develop our faith in Him by revealing just one step at a time. We have to trust Him in such times of uncertainty and patiently walk through each door of opportunity that He opens.*

5. *Encourage the group members to come up with specific opportunities—opportunities to which they said yes, or opportunities they failed to notice at the time. Evaluating their days in this manner is a useful way to develop the skill of noticing these moments when they come.*

6. *Developing a habit of seeking Jesus in the small things is much like learning to play a musical instrument or a sport. In the beginning, it doesn't feel natural to look to Him in the small things. Our minds wander; or other, "more urgent" matters arise that require our attention; or we simply forget to seek Him. But if we persist, we can overcome these obstacles and improve at focusing on Jesus for longer periods of time—and, as a result, we will more naturally turn to Him in times of trouble. Even something as simple as saying His name every fifteen minutes can help us develop the habit of regularly returning our thoughts to Him.*

7. *Job is making the point that people go to so much trouble digging mines for useful metals and precious stones—but fewer people put that much effort into seeking wisdom. He likely uses so many statements to make the point because he is imagining the effort required in mining. If we've never been in a mine, we might take for granted how much trouble goes into finding metals and digging them out of the deep earth. So, through Job's words, the Lord takes us into the mine itself and makes us think about the effort. Then Job raises key questions about wisdom: Where can it be found? Do we know? Do we take it for granted the way we take mined materials for granted?*

8. *Job says that wisdom is priceless. It cannot be bought, even with the things we think are so valuable, like gold and jewels. God may have again piled on the images so we would really think about this truth and not brush past it quickly. The Lord's wisdom can't be bought for any sum of money. It can't be acquired by any means—not even with all our technology and know-how. It is far more valuable than these things. So for any effort we put into obtaining money or possessions, we should put far more effort into obtaining wisdom.*

9. *"Fear of the Lord" means to take Him seriously and treat Him as the King of kings who should be first in our thoughts and lives. As Jesus would later state, it means to "love the Lord your God with all your heart and with all your soul and with all your strength and with all your mind" (Luke 10:27). Developing this kind of godly fear will help believers during times of uncertainty by reminding us that God is in sovereign control of our circumstances—and we need to seek His will on what course to take.*

10. *We often approach the question of God's will as if it were a question of how to make our lives work so we will be happy. But the fear of the Lord reveals the truth: wisdom is more about making choices that lead to holiness. Putting Jesus first won't necessarily make things feel good to us all the time, but it will make us fruitful and intimate with Him . . . and that is far more fulfilling in the long run.*

11. *Answers will vary.*

12. *Answers will vary.*

13. *Responses will vary.*

Session 5: Putting Jesus First in Times of Longing

1. *There are many types of longings and "thirsts" that people have today, including the core desires for love, security, understanding, purpose, significance, and belonging. While these longings are not wrong in and of themselves, it is important to put Jesus first when we seek to fill them. As we do, we will find that our longings begin to shift from the desire to fulfill our own wants to the desire to pursue the greater things of God.*

2. *Allow group members to provide examples of how they have seen people try to fulfill personal longings—but briefly, and without mentioning names. The goal is to simply point out the problem of seeking to fill our longings* *outside of Christ, whether by pursuing relationships, seeking control over things beyond our control, or blindly following after what we think will make us feel successful and desired.*

3. *Resting in Jesus can be a form of worship because by it, we declare that Jesus is in charge and He will ensure that everything important gets done. It is an act that dethrones productivity as a false god. Worship also allows us to enter into God's presence and focus on Him rather than our own wants. As we do this, God fills us and meets our deeper needs.*

4. *The truth is that Jesus doesn't want us to drive ourselves into the ground in the constant pursuit to fulfill our longings. Rather, He states, "Come to me, all you who are weary and burdened, and I will give you rest" (Matthew 11:28). Of course, driving ourselves so hard can be a tough habit to break, especially for parents with small children, who require so much attention. At the other end of the spectrum, we need to make sure we're not "resting" by consuming an inordinate amount of entertainment. Resting in Netflix or Facebook is not the same as resting in Jesus!*

5. *Some examples include the desire to be loved—to have intimacy and connection—which is fulfilled more deeply in Jesus than in any human relationship. This is something we discover over time as we rest in Jesus' presence. The desire for joy is fulfilled in Him more than in any earthly experience. The desire for significance is fulfilled when we receive guidance from Christ about what we were made for and He empowers us to do what we couldn't do on our own.*

6. *The temptation to be self-sufficient and self-confident is alluring because we think we will receive more respect from others if we are perceived as being strong. Paul's statement that the Lord will "delight in weaknesses . . . for when I am weak, then I am strong" (2 Corinthians 12:10) is counterintuitive to us. But ultimately, God has designed us to be dependent on Him and to find our strength and worth in Him alone.*

7. *People "spend money on what is not bread" by pursuing the lesser things of this world (such as money, control, and success) over Jesus. They do this because the world tells them these things will satisfy their longings—as just about any product advertisement promises. These lesser things may produce short-term satisfaction in people, but in time the hunger for something deeper sets in.*

8. *Even for Christians, we can't obey Jesus and receive fulfillment from Him unless we are listening closely to what He is asking us to do. Also, listening is a prime element of a genuine relationship. In prayer we talk (and are hopefully listening for the Holy Spirit), but do we listen for how God is guiding us through His Word? That's what Jesus asks us to do. Are we reading the Scriptures and heeding what He has said?*

9. *An example of a human thought would be,* It's up to me to get this task done the right way, *which in our terms means "the way that looks perfect to me." Contrast this to Jesus' thoughts, which could be,* It's not up to you to get this done your way. It's up to you to depend on Me, and My way is considerate of other people's needs and desires. My way is loving and peaceful and patient.

10. *The final reason we find in this passage is because Jesus' word never fails. He always accomplishes the purpose for which He speaks something into being. Thus, if we set our hearts on the things He desires—above all else and before anything else—we will never be disappointed.*

11. *Answers will vary.*

12. *Answers will vary.*

13. *Responses will vary.*

Session 6: Putting Jesus First in Relationships

1. *What you're aiming for here is a picture of each group member's family dynamic. Some of them may be caring for children, others may have grown children but parents who need care, and others may have responsibility for multiple generations. Caregiving is much more effective when we are able to put Jesus first in each of these relationships.*

2. *Answers will vary. Children are generally treated with more love and fairness in homes where Jesus comes first than in homes where the children come first. And homes where parents are pursuing their own selfish agendas leave deep scars.*

3. *Some signs that a loved one might be an idol are: favoring that person over others, trying to shield that loved one from the consequences of his or her actions, or if we willingly disobey or shortchange God in order to please that person.*

4. *We can literally endanger our loved ones if we make them more important to us than Jesus. (We'll see in this week's Bible study just how that played out for Joseph when his father put him first.) Sometimes we have to entrust someone to Jesus again and again because we're inclined to worry about him or her. This is fundamentally a trust issue between us and the Lord. We know we've entrusted our loved one to Christ's care when the anxious thoughts, the favoritism, and the rescuing stop.*

5. *If God is truly the First Love in our lives, we will feel compelled to spend time with Him each day in prayer. We will desire to dive into His Word to connect with Him and understand how He wants us to live. As we do this, we will find ourselves being concerned about the things that concern* Him *more than we are concerned for our own personal desires. We will be willing to be "inconvenienced" for God and take steps of faith as He leads us. And we will* *be motivated to share His love and the hope we have found in Christ with others.*

6. *When we view Jesus as the Master of our lives, it changes our entire perspective on our relationships. This could affect the amount of time we spend with our friends and family—we make time to be with Jesus rather than giving our loved ones all of our attention. It could affect the way we treat our loved ones, for we understand that Jesus wants us to love them as He loves us. It could also affect the reasons we do things for others: to serve them out of love instead of obligation or a desire to earn their favor.*

7. *Jacob/Israel created family tension by giving Joseph an ornate robe (also known as "a coat of many colors"). While there are various interpretations as to what this robe signified, it was definitely a sign that Jacob favored Joseph above his other sons. While this favoritism had likely been building for some time, this gift seems to have been the tipping point that set off Joseph's brothers, judging by their consequent actions. Parents do still sometimes favor one child over another, but we need to be careful not to act on that favoritism, lest it lead to consequences as it did in Jacob's household.*

8. *Joseph showed his immaturity by telling his brothers the dream he had—and that dream involved them bowing before him. Even though the dream was a prophecy of events to come, it was not necessary (or helpful) for Joseph to share it at the time. His inability to keep quiet, coupled with the gift of the ornate robe, seems to have stirred the brothers to act against him.*

9. *Joseph's brothers talked about killing him or letting him rot in an empty cistern, but they finally settled on selling him into slavery. It's an extreme case of sibling rivalry, but even in today's world, there are families that do extreme things when the parents aren't putting God first and haven't taught their children to do so. Troubles of all kinds arise between siblings in a household where God is perhaps acknowledged but Jesus doesn't rule in people's hearts.*

10. *Not everyone in the group will have played favorites in the family. However, most of us have probably been guilty at one time or another of putting family before Jesus. Family needs are so obvious, while Jesus is easy to set aside. We have to make a determined effort to put Jesus first in order to keep this from happening.*

11. *Answers will vary.*

12. *Answers will vary.*

13. *Responses will vary.*

Session 7: Putting Jesus First in Finances

1. *For this question, you are sure to get a variety of responses from group members. Expect to hear words such as "scarcity," "obligation," "burden," or "difficulties" to indicate the stress many of them feel when thinking about money—and the apparent lack of it in their lives. Others may use words such as "opportunity," "tool," or "steward" to show they view money as a means of helping others. Some may use words such as "blessing," "abundance," and "gift" to show they view money as a gift from God.*

2. *It's likely that money plays a prominent role in the group members' lives—just as it played a significant role in people's lives when Jesus was on the earth. Almost everyone struggles with feeling we don't have enough money to meet our needs or to enable us to do what we want to do. But the Bible urges us to view money as a gift that comes to us from God. The money is His—and He has entrusted it to us to fulfill His purposes. This shift in our mindset can make us more generous with others, less stressed about money, and more grateful for everything.*

3. *Money is a sensitive subject for most of us, and we typically don't want to be transparent with* anyone *about the way we deal with it or how we view it.*

Like anybody else, Christians often struggle to trust God when money is tight and battle complacency when money is sufficient. As the leader, be ready to set the example by talking honestly about how you speak with Jesus about money and how you would like to interact with Him about it.

4. *Money is an unreliable source of peace because circumstances can so quickly snatch it away. A long illness or job loss can suddenly and severely impact our finances. Even if we have enough money to meet our needs, we are prone to worry about losing our wealth or compete with others for status if we don't trust Jesus. Yet as He said, we can't serve both God and money.*

5. *In Matthew 19:24, Jesus made the startling statement that "it is easier for a camel to go through the eye of a needle than for someone who is rich to enter the kingdom of God." Money often makes people more selfish and self-reliant. When we lack money, it can enable us to look to God rather than to ourselves to provide for our needs—if we let it. It may also motivate us to live in the present moment, not in the uncertain future. None of this is easy to do, but we can make progress each day just by choosing to say, "Jesus, I trust You."*

6. *You will likely have some group members who are able to talk about sudden downturns in their health or the health of a family member, or sudden demands on their budgets that they weren't expecting. If they're honest, some might say those experiences made them trust Jesus less. But Jesus never promised smooth sailing for His followers—on the contrary, He promised we would encounter difficulties in the world (see John 16:33). Hopefully, most in the group will have weathered the storms and, through their experiences, learned to depend on Jesus more than they had before.*

7. *The economy was bad! The Jews were primarily farmers, and they were facing a drought that made the harvests fail. Their livestock were also suffering. The people were working hard, but they were not seeing the abundance they expected and needed.*

8. *It was a mistake because it indicated their lack of trust and dependence on the Lord. God was sending the hard times to show His people that self-sufficiency was a myth. He wanted them to exercise their faith through obedience—by devoting their time and resources to getting the timber to build a house of worship, just as He had instructed them to do.*

9. *We, like the Israelites, are often tempted to give less money to the work of God when times are bad. It's natural for us to think we should pay our bills and then consider what we can "afford" to give back to God, but the truth is that giving first to Him shows the condition of our hearts—and that we view Him as the true Owner of all that we have (see Psalm 50:9–12).*

10. *Jesus said, "Where your treasure is, there your heart will be also" (Matthew 6:21). Putting Jesus first with our finances is, at its core, a matter of the attitude of our hearts. Jesus wants us to love Him more than we love money and live in gratitude for His gifts, not in frustration that we don't have more. He also wants us to understand that our spending and saving reflect our hearts, as does our stewardship of all the resources He gives us, such as our time and talents.*

11. *Answers will vary.*

12. *Answers will vary.*

13. *Responses will vary.*

Session 8: Putting Jesus First and Serving Him Alone

1. *There are many types of idols that people worship today. Some bow to the idol of materialism, acquiring more and more possessions, which builds their feelings of self-worth. Others idolize celebrities, coveting their lavish lifestyles. Many bow to the idol of pride (in the form of obsession with work, success, or status) in order to elevate themselves. Some bow to the idol of pleasure,* *pursuing fulfillment through entertainment, distractions (like social media), or anything else that makes them feel good in the moment. Some even bow to the idol of rules, much like the Pharisees in the Bible who loved God's laws more than God's people (see Matthew 23:1–12).*

2. *Answers will vary. As the leader, consider answering this question first. It's a more vulnerable question than is usual for an icebreaker, but your group has been meeting for several weeks now and is hopefully ready for it. Make your group a safe place for people to be honest.*

3. *Our minds can be occupied by thoughts of work, busy schedules, food, anxiety, children, household tasks, goals, achievements, bank accounts—any of these things can drive out thoughts of Jesus. Help members identify their dominant thoughts at the present time and be willing to admit them within the safety of the group.*

4. *Jesus wants us to break free from bondage by affirming our trust in Him and refreshing ourselves in His presence. Shaking off the allure of idols begins by spending time with Jesus and refocusing our thoughts on Him as the foundation of our lives. We choose to do this again and again until it becomes habit.*

5. *The key consideration is whether we are talking to Jesus about our goal and submitting it to His will. We must carefully think through and pray to discern if Jesus wants us to have this thing that we are pursuing, or if we are driving for it in our own strength and for our own purposes.*

6. *We don't know whether we're going to get the thing we desire, and we don't know whether it's something Jesus wants us to have. As the situation unfolds, however, Jesus will make those things clear to His followers—if we are paying attention to Him and staying in communication with Him. Invite your group members to be honest about their desires.*

7. *Isaiah told the people that if they chose to follow God, the Lord would be gracious to them when they cried out for help and answer them immediately. While God didn't say they would lead an adversity-free existence—and we too may have to drink from the "water of affliction"—He did promise to guide their way. In the end, the people of Israel would realize their idols were worthless and they would throw them away.*

8. *It's important to remember that we don't need "special words" from the Lord about the path we should take, because He has already laid out the course in His Word. Passages of Scripture such as Matthew 5–7; Romans 12; and Ephesians 4–6 provide practical guidance for how to live. Try to help your group identify those things about which Jesus has already spoken, and then discuss their particular questions for their lives.*

9. *In the passage, God promises to provide abundant food, water, and sunshine. These were especially meaningful to the prophecy's first hearers, as they were about to face a siege and the likelihood that their food supplies would be cut off. As believers, we can likewise look forward to having our deepest needs met when we trust Jesus enough to throw away our idols.*

10. *It's more difficult during times of adversity because our idols often provide immediate and tangible relief from our circumstances. When hard times come, we may start to think that Jesus isn't coming through for us, so we turn to idols to ease our pain. But idols will only make life worse. Jesus alone offers the trustworthy voice that says, "This is the way; walk in it."*

11. *Answers will vary.*

12. *Answers will vary.*

13. *Responses will vary.*

Also Available in the Jesus Calling® Bible Study Series

Also Available in the Jesus Calling® Bible Study Series